PEARL HARBOR

STEPHANIE FITZGERALD

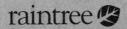

raintree

a Capstone company — publishers for children

Raintree is an imprint of Capstone Global Library Limited, a company incorporated in England and Wales having its registered office at 264 Banbury Road, Oxford, OX2 7DY – Registered company number: 6695582

www.raintree.co.uk
myorders@raintree.co.uk

Editorial Credits
Sarah Bennett, Jaclyn Jaycox, Angela Kaelberer, Kelli Lageson, Kathy McColley and Catherine Neitge
Originated by Capstone Global Library Limited
Printed and bound in China.

ISBN 978 1 4747 4319 8
21 20 19 18 17
10 9 8 7 6 5 4 3 2 1

British Library Cataloguing in Publication Data
A full catalogue record for this book is available from the British Library.

Acknowledgements
Alamy: GL Archive, 8, 79, PJF Military Collection, 36; Bridgeman Images: Don Troiani, 50; Getty Images: Corbis Historical, 56, Roger-Viollet, 51; Library of Congress, cover, 30, 47, 54; National Archives and Records Administration: 2, 14, 25, 26, 33, 40, 58, 67, 68, 72, 75, 80, 82, 85, 87, 88, 93, 97, 100, 101 (left and right), 102 (left), 103 (top and bottom left); Newscom: Photoshot/UPAA, 22, 48, 90, Pictures from History, 29, POOL/Jiji Press, 99; Shutterstock: Everett Historical, 6, 13, 18, 20, 21, 52, Ivan Cholakov, 45; US Navy Photo: 11, 39, 41, 42 (top and bottom), 61, 63, 64; Wikimedia: Hiromichi Matsuda, 103 (bottom right); XNR Productions: 17, 59

CONTENTS

The USS *Shaw* exploded after it was bombed by Japanese pilots during the attack on Pearl Harbor.

CHAPTER ONE

SURPRISE ATTACK

Dave Smith woke up at about 7.30 a.m. on the morning of 7 December 1941. Smith was a US navy seaman apprentice serving aboard the battleship USS *Utah*. The ship was docked at Pearl Harbor naval base on the Hawaiian island of Oahu. Wearing only his boxer shorts, Smith left his cabin and walked up to his locker on the old gun deck. He was going to get dressed, but he never got the chance.

Smith was surprised to hear the sound of an aeroplane. It was Sunday morning, and most of the sailors and pilots stationed at the base weren't working that day. He looked out of a porthole and saw a plane flying towards him, just above the surface of the ocean. Smith thought the pilot was taking part in a training

The USS *Utah* was one of five US battleships sunk during the attack on Pearl Harbor.

drill. Just then, a torpedo dropped from the plane and slammed into the ship. As the plane climbed, Smith could see a large red circle under each of its wings. Suddenly he understood. This was no training exercise – the plane was Japanese, and Pearl Harbor was under attack!

The *Utah* wasn't the only battleship at Pearl Harbor that morning. Ford Island, which was the site of the

Naval Air Station and patrol and utility plane hangars, is in the centre of the harbour. The waters off Ford Island are deep. That area, known as Battleship Row, is where the USS *California*, USS *Maryland*, USS *Oklahoma*, USS *Tennessee*, USS *West Virginia*, USS *Arizona* and USS *Nevada* were positioned. The *Utah* was across the harbour on the west side of Ford Island. Another battleship, the USS *Pennsylvania*, was in the navy yard's dry dock for repairs. Two destroyers, the USS *Cassin* and the USS *Downes*, were also in the dry dock.

Smith yelled a warning to his fellow sailors. He decided to go up to the main deck, one deck above the gun deck. He crawled up the ladder and then made his way on his hands and knees to where he could see the harbour. "I could see the battleships on the other side of Ford Island taking hits, blowing up and burning. Commander [Solomon] Isquith was there and said for everyone to put on a life jacket and prepare to abandon ship," he said later.

Smith saw fuel pouring from the *Utah*'s damaged fuel tanks into the harbour. He decided to swim underwater to Ford Island to try to avoid the oil. He took off his life jacket, slid down the side of the capsizing ship and swam for his life. "When I reached the island and looked back," he said, "all I saw was the bottom of the *Utah*."

Smith was fortunate – he survived the terrible attack, which lasted less than two hours. But 2,403 other Americans, including 68 civilians, weren't so lucky. They were killed in the attack. Among them were 58 sailors aboard the *Utah*. Another 1,178 member of the military and civilians were wounded. It was one of the deadliest days in navy history. Twenty-one ships were sunk or damaged, 188 aircraft were destroyed and 159 aircraft were damaged. Most of the planes were hit before they could take off.

As bombs and torpedoes rocked the ships on Battleship Row, sailors were thrown from their bunks, and some were blown off the decks into the water. The bombs and

torpedoes ripped huge holes in the ships' hulls, sending

water rushing into the living quarters. As sailors closed

Ford Island was at the centre of the attack when Japanese bombers dropped bombs and torpedoes on US battleships and aircraft below.

THE *UTAH*

The USS *Utah* was one of five battleships sunk during the 7 December 1941, attack on Pearl Harbor. Today, though, many people aren't familiar with its story.

The *Utah* was commissioned in 1911. By October 1941 the navy had made the aging battleship a target ship. Navy officials planned to use it as a mock enemy warship during training exercises. As part of the refurbishing, the *Utah* had new guns and armour. The Japanese pilots may have mistaken the *Utah* for an aircraft carrier, even though no carriers were at Pearl Harbor that day.

The first of two Japanese torpedoes hit the *Utah* at 8.01 a.m. Within minutes, the ship's senior officer, Lieutenant Commander Solomon Isquith, ordered the crew to abandon ship. Most of the crew – 461 sailors – made it to safety. By 8.12 a.m. the ship's mooring lines had snapped and the ship had capsized. Of the 58 crew members killed during the attack, only 4 were recovered. The other 54 bodies are still in the sunken ship.

The other battleships sunk at Pearl Harbor were the USS *Arizona*, USS *California*, USS *West Virginia* and USS *Oklahoma*. The *Oklahoma* was later recovered and sold for scrap. The wreck of the *Arizona* remains in the harbour waters and serves as a memorial. It is visited by 1.5 million people each year. Dedicated in 1962, the USS *Arizona* Memorial straddles the sunken ship. The memorial lists the names of the sailors on the ship who were killed that day.

The *Utah*'s wreckage is also still at Pearl Harbor, marked by a small memorial. Only people with military identification are allowed to visit it.

The sunken USS *Arizona* is the final resting place for many of the 1,177 crew members who were killed during the attack.

and locked watertight doors to keep out the water, they became trapped inside the burning, sinking ships.

Within moments, all of the ships on Battleship Row had been hit with torpedoes, bombs or both. The harbour's waters were slick with oil, and thick, black smoke filled the sky. Fires killed many sailors who survived the first explosions. Others who made it into

A group of unarmed B-17s flying from California, USA, unknowingly flew right into the attack. Some were damaged while landing at Hickam Field near the Pearl Harbor naval base.

the water couldn't swim to safety. The weight of their uniforms dragged them down, and the oil made their skin so slippery it was hard for rescuers to pull them from the water.

At the same time, Japanese bombers were attacking the airfields scattered across the island. Within minutes, many of the planes were destroyed, along with barracks, fire stations and fire engines.

Japan's sneak attack on Pearl Harbor was a huge military victory. It helped the Japanese to dominate the war in the Pacific for at least six months while the US Navy rebuilt and repaired its fleet. But the attack was also a major political mistake. Before the attack, most Americans weren't in favour of the United States entering into World War II. Japan's actions angered the American people and spurred them to completely support the war.

PEARL HARBOR BEFORE THE ATTACK

Pearl Harbor is a lagoon on the southern coast of Oahu island in Hawaii. The US Navy took possession of the harbour in 1887 under a treaty between the United States and Hawaii. After the United States annexed Hawaii in 1898, the navy began adding to its installations on the islands. The Pearl Harbor naval base was established in 1908 and its dry dock was completed in 1919. By 1934 the base included aeroplanes and submarines.

In 1940 the US Pacific Fleet held training exercises at Pearl Harbor, which became the fleet's permanent home in February 1941. South-east of Ford Island were the navy base, the hospital and Hickam Field Army Air Base. The Ewa Field Marine Corps air base was across the entrance from Hickam, and Wheeler Airfield was north of Pearl Harbor in the centre of Oahu. The base was so big that the entire US Navy fleet could dock, get fuel and supplies, and be repaired all at once, in one place.

About 17,500 men and 200 women were stationed at Pearl Harbor in December 1941. Most of the women served as nurses. In the 1930s and 1940s air travel was expensive, and few people travelled far from their homes. Many of the young men and women stationed at Pearl Harbor had never been away from their homes before, and few had been to a place as exotic as Oahu. With its sunny skies, sandy

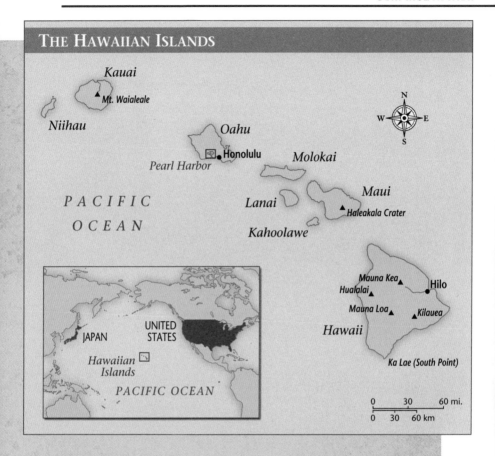

THE HAWAIIAN ISLANDS

Kauai

▲ Mt. Waialeale

Niihau

Oahu

Honolulu

Pearl Harbor

Molokai

PACIFIC

OCEAN

Lanai

Maui

▲ Haleakala Crater

Kahoolawe

Mauna Kea ▲

Hualalai ▲

Hilo

Mauna Loa ▲

▲ Kilauea

Hawaii

Ka Lae (South Point)

JAPAN

UNITED
STATES

Hawaiian
Islands

PACIFIC OCEAN

| 0 | 30 | 60 mi. |
| 0 | 30 | 60 km |

beaches and warm ocean waters, Oahu was, and is, a popular holiday destination.

During a typical week, sailors on the battleships practised manoeuvres and firing drills. Pilots took part in firing and bombing exercises. The hospital nurses treated patients whose complaints were rarely worse than a bad case of sunburn. Weekends were for relaxing. On Saturday nights people went to dances and the cinema. Sundays were for sleeping late, attending church and playing sport such as baseball or golf.

Japanese soldiers celebrated the capture of Nanking, China, in 1937. However, their brutal attacks on the men, women and children in China increased the tension between Japan and the United States.

CHAPTER TWO

THE ROAD TO PEARL HARBOR

Why did Japan attack the United States? The answer goes back to at least 10 years before the Pearl Harbor bombing.

In 1931 Japan invaded the Manchuria region of China. China was much larger than Japan, but it was going through a civil war that weakened its ability to defend itself. Japan had few natural resources and wanted to expand its empire to include countries that did have these resources. The government especially wanted to obtain nickel, iron, tin, oil and rubber – all materials that were needed for war.

Encouraged by Japan's successful invasion of Manchuria, Japanese leaders continued to move on northern China. By 1937, China and Japan were involved in the brutal Second Sino-Japanese War (1937–1945). Japanese troops tortured and murdered more than 250,000 men, women and children in the Nanking region of China. In response, the United States increased its military and financial aid to China. The United States also increased its military power in the Pacific and stopped supplying Japan with oil and other raw materials, which angered Japanese leaders.

The Second Sino-Japanese War was the most significant war in Asia in the 20th century and eventually merged into World War II.

Germany bombed London for 57 consecutive days and nights during what became known as the Blitz.

On 1 September 1939, Germany invaded Poland, which started World War II (1939–1945) in Europe. Britain and France quickly declared war on Germany, but the United States didn't follow their lead. Germany continued to invade and conquer other countries in Europe, including Belgium, the Netherlands and France. Though many countries tried to stop the invading forces, only Britain was able to resist them. But Germany was bombing British cities every night in air attacks known as the Blitz, destroying homes and factories and killing thousands of British civilians.

The British hoped that the United States would enter the war and help them to defeat the Germans.

Germany, however, had gained its own allies. On 27 September 1940, Japan signed the Tripartite Pact with Germany and Italy to form the Axis alliance. The three nations pledged to help each other with military, economic and political issues.

The Tripartite Pact signing ceremony in Berlin included (seated, from left) Japan's Ambassador Saburō Kurusu, Italy's Minister of Foreign Affairs Galeazzo Ciano and Germany's Führer Adolf Hitler.

Japan decided to obtain natural resources from the countries and territories of Southeast Asia. But the United States also controlled parts of Southeast Asia, including the Philippines, Samoa, Guam, Wake Island and Hawaii. US leaders didn't want Japan to take over the US territories. They were also worried that Japan would block them from trading with the Chinese.

In September 1940 Japan invaded French Indochina. This area today includes the countries of Vietnam, Laos and Cambodia. Chinese and British troops in Southeast Asia were causing problems with Japan's plans to conquer the area. But the Japanese government saw that the US Pacific Fleet stationed at Pearl Harbor was the only thing really standing in its way.

By early 1941 the relationship between Japan and the United States had reached boiling point. Peace talks between the two nations began in February of that year, but officials on both sides found it very difficult to agree on anything. The United States wanted Japan to stop taking over other Asian nations. Japan refused.

LEND-LEASE ACT

Because of US laws called Neutrality Acts that were passed in the late 1930s, the United States could only provide weapons and war materials on a "cash and carry" basis to other countries that were at war. But when Britain was unable to pay cash for war materials, US President Franklin D. Roosevelt came up with the idea for the Lend-Lease Act.

The new law allowed the United States to simply transfer war materials to its allies, rather than selling them. By the end of the war, the United States had provided about 50 billion US dollars in aid to more than 40 countries. It was up to the president to decide how each country would repay the United States. Most countries were released from repaying their war debts.

Despite what was happening in Europe and the Pacific, most US citizens didn't support entering the war. They were isolationists – they felt that the war in Europe didn't concern them. By the end of 1941, however, that would all change.

Weapons were sent to Britain, China, the Soviet Union and many other countries under the Lend-Lease Act.

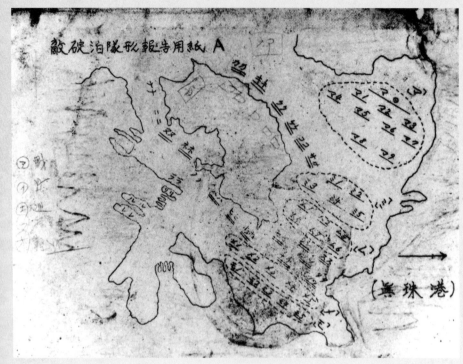

A chart recovered from a downed Japanese aircraft during the attack on Pearl Harbor mapped out the locations of US battleships and aircraft.

CHAPTER THREE

PLANS FOR THE ATTACK

By spring 1941 the United States had made its position with Japan clear. Secretary of State Cordell Hull was meeting regularly in Washington, DC, with Kichisaburo Nomura, Japan's ambassador to the United States. Hull insisted that Japan needed to remove its 1 million troops occupying China and withdraw from the Tripartite Pact with Germany and Italy. Japanese government leaders didn't agree to do those things.

Japan's leaders met on 6 September 1941, to discuss the possibility of war with the United States. Not all agreed that a war was a good idea, including Prime Minister Fuminaro Konoe. But in October, Army Minister Hideki Tojo replaced Konoe as prime minister. While Japan's emperor is technically the head of the government, the prime minister is actually the person in charge of the executive branch. Tojo supported going to war against the United States, and now he had the power to make that happen.

The idea to attack Pearl Harbor came from Admiral Isoroku Yamamoto, commander of the Japanese fleet. Yamamoto knew more about the United States than most Japanese leaders. He had studied at Harvard University in the United States for two years and later served as a representative of the Japanese navy in Washington, DC.

Yamamoto was impressed with the United States' industrial power and knew how effective it would be in fighting a war. He believed that the Japanese could only cause major damage to the US military with a surprise attack. But he also realized the attack wouldn't permanently disable the US fleet. And he didn't think Japan could win a long war with the United States. In September 1940 he told Prime Minister Konoe, "In the first six to twelve months of a war with the United States and Britain I will run wild and win victory upon

RELUCTANT WARRIOR

Isoroku Yamamoto, who planned the Pearl Harbor attack down to its last detail, was born in 1884 into the large Takano family. His first name means "56", which was his father's age when he was born. After his parents died, the Yamamoto family adopted Isoroku, even though he was 32 years old. The Yamamoto family had no sons and needed one to carry on the family name, which was very important in Japanese society at that time.

Yamamoto graduated from the Imperial Japanese Naval Academy in 1904, and by 1930 he held the rank of rear admiral. He opposed many of Japan's military actions during the 1930s, including the invasion of Manchuria and the subsequent war with China. He also spoke out against the Tripartite Pact with Germany and Italy. But despite his unpopular ideas, he became navy vice minister in 1936 and commander in chief of the combined fleet in 1939.

After the attack on Pearl Harbor, Yamamoto led the Imperial Navy during the Battle of Midway in June 1942, which ended in an Allied victory. US pilots shot down an aeroplane carrying Yamamoto on 18 April 1943, killing all aboard.

THE EMPEROR'S ROLE

Although Japan had a prime minister, its emperor still had a great deal of power at the time of World War II. In fact, the Japanese people considered their emperors living gods.

Emperor Hirohito was born in 1901 and took over duties from his father, Yoshihito, in 1921. He became emperor in 1926 after Yoshihito's death from illness. No one is sure how much Hirohito was involved with Japan's military decisions before and during the war. It's believed he wasn't pleased with the army's brutal actions during its invasion of China, but he refused to punish its members. In 1941 he approved the Imperial Navy's plan to attack Pearl Harbor.

After the war ended in 1945, Japan's new constitution reduced Hirohito's role to ceremonial duties only. He died in 1989 after the longest reign in Japanese history.

victory. But then, if the war continues after that, I have no expectation of success."

Yamamoto's plan, called Operation Z or Operation Hawaii, focused on the Japanese navy's six aircraft carriers. In spring 1941 the aircraft carrier crews began training for a surprise attack. They learned how to refuel at sea – something that had never been done before. Pilots practised taking off from carrier decks in choppy waves. They lowered their altitude for dropping bombs from 610 metres (2,000 feet) to 457 metres (1,500 feet) for greater accuracy.

Operation Z didn't get immediate approval from other Japanese military leaders. Some wanted a more conservative plan to engage the United States in war, such as invading Southeast Asia in the hopes that the United States would try to intervene. But in October 1941 the Japanese naval leaders gave their final approval to Operation Z. The navy formed a task force commanded by Vice Admiral Chuichi Nagumo. Navy Air Service Captain Mitsuo Fuchida served under Nagumo and was put in charge of the air attack.

Even though the plan was approved, the attack wasn't certain to go ahead. After much debate, Japan's government and military leaders agreed that Foreign Minister Shigenori Togo and Ambassador Nomura would have until midnight on 30 November to try to negotiate peace terms with the United States. The leaders presented the approved attack plan to Emperor Hirohito on 2 November, however. Hirohito was unsure at first that an attack was necessary but, after more discussion, he agreed, saying, "Perhaps it is unavoidable that we continue preparations for military operations."

Japan's naval planners decided that "X-Day" – the day of the attack – would be Monday 8 December. Because of different time zones, the date in Hawaii would be Sunday 7 December. Sunday is a holy day for the Christian religion, and many of the US sailors were Christian. Japanese leaders knew that all of the US ships would be at anchor and most of the military members would be off duty that morning.

They also knew the attack would only work if it took the US Navy by surprise. The Japanese naval high command could call back Nagumo's strike force as late as 6 December. After that, Nagumo would have to decide whether to continue the attack.

In the last week of November, Nagumo's fleet gathered in Tankan Bay in the Kuril Islands, which are between Japan and Russia. The fleet included six aircraft carriers: *Akagi, Kaga, Soryu, Hiryu, Shokaku* and *Zuikaku*. The carriers held a total of more than 420 aeroplanes. Sailing with the carriers were 24 supporting ships –

Japanese planes prepared to take off from an aircraft carrier to attack Pearl Harbor.

battleships, destroyers, cruisers and tankers – and a group of submarines to sink any US ships that escaped the harbour. The fleet began its journey to Hawaii on 26 November.

To keep its mission a secret, the fleet used a North Pacific route that wasn't used much in the winter because of the chance of bad weather such as rough seas and heavy fog. To avoid being overheard by the Americans, the Japanese sailors couldn't use their radios. The ships could only communicate using flashing lights and flags.

Japanese leaders decided on 1 December not to accept the peace terms proposed by the United States. But Japan didn't declare war on the United States then. Togo and Nomura indicated to US leaders that the peace talks would continue – even as the final decision to attack Pearl Harbor was made.

On 2 December, Admiral Yamamoto radioed a message to the strike force: Climb Mount Niitaka 1208. That was the code for "proceed with attack". By dawn on 7 December, the fleet was about 320 kilometres (200 miles) north of Oahu. The Americans had no idea what was about to hit them.

CHANCE MEETING AT SEA

The Japanese strike force chose its route wisely. The fleet met just one foreign vessel during its journey. The Soviet trawler *Uritsky* encountered the fleet on 5 December. The Japanese allowed the *Uritsky* to pass and, apparently, the Soviet crew repaid the favour by not notifying the United States. Soviet leaders probably guessed that the Japanese fleet was heading for Pearl Harbor. At the time, the Soviet Union was at war with Germany, which had invaded the Soviet Union in June 1941. But the Soviet Union wasn't yet at war with Japan. If the United States entered the war on the side of the Allies, this would be beneficial to the Soviet Union. It may be that the Soviet leaders chose to keep quiet, believing that an attack on the US base would encourage the United States to join the war.

A 1940 aerial view of Pearl Harbor

CHAPTER FOUR

BEFORE THE ATTACK

One question people still ask is, "Did the United States have any idea that a Japanese attack on Pearl Harbor was coming?" Although the answer is unclear, US leaders definitely knew in 1941 that Japan was a threat. The US military had broken the secret code that Japanese leaders used to communicate their plans. The Japanese discussed very little in secret messages that the Americans didn't know about. And US ambassadors around the world passed information they heard about the Japanese to US government leaders.

Government and military leaders, however, were wrong about one very important thing – the attack's location. They thought the Japanese would be much more likely to attack US Navy bases in the Philippines or

SPIES IN HAWAII

US leaders did have one concern about Hawaii. They feared that Japanese citizens living on the islands were spying for Japan. There was good reason for that concern – some Japanese spies were posing as tourists or working in low-level jobs at a Japanese diplomatic office in Honolulu. One spy was Takeo Yoshikawa, a former Japanese navy officer who worked as a clerk under the name of Tadashi Morimura. In his free time, Yoshikawa swam and fished in the harbour and went to clubs and restaurants frequented by US officers. "Sometimes I went around Pearl Harbor by taxi or bus. Sometimes I walked along, drinking a beer, to get information. I did, you know, 'fishing' to mark the depths of the sea," he said later.

Guam. Both places are much closer to Japan than Hawaii. Nobody thought Japanese ships could carry enough fuel to sail to Hawaii and back – a one-way distance of 6,196 kilometres (3,850 miles). Likewise, no one thought a large strike force would be able to sail from Japan to Hawaii without being discovered. US Navy leaders warned the bases in the Philippines and Guam and strengthened defences there. Submarines were stationed around other military bases in the Pacific, including Wake and Midway islands, for protection.

But some leaders thought Pearl Harbor might be a target. Early in 1941, Rear Admiral Richmond Kelly Turner wrote these eerily prophetic words in a letter to Secretary of War Henry L. Stimson, which was signed by Turner's boss, Secretary of the Navy Fred Knox: "If war eventuates with Japan, it is believed easily possible that hostilities would be initiated by a surprise attack upon the Fleet or the Naval Base at Pearl Harbor." Apparently Stimson didn't take Turner's opinion seriously.

A stronger warning came just 10 days before the attack. Admiral Husband Kimmel, the commander of the Pacific Fleet, received a message from the Navy Department. It read in part: "This dispatch is to be considered a war warning. Negotiations with Japan

Admiral Husband Kimmel was removed from his command 10 days after the attack.

[. . .] have ceased and an aggressive move by Japan is expected within the next few days." The message listed the Philippines, Thailand and Borneo as possible targets – but not Hawaii.

While the attack came as a surprise, there were some indications early in the morning of 7 December that things weren't quite normal. The US destroyer *Ward* and two minesweepers, *Condor* and *Crossbill*, were patrolling the entrance to Pearl Harbor when an officer on the *Condor*, R.C. McCloy, saw what he thought was a submarine periscope. The crew quickly sent a message

The *Condor* was believed to have made the first enemy contact on the morning of 7 December 1941.

40

The *Ward's* crew was the first to fire at enemy invaders.

to the *Ward*. The *Ward's* crew members woke the captain, Lieutenant William Outerbridge, who searched the area for about an hour without seeing a periscope. Because they couldn't confirm that McCloy had seen a periscope, neither ship reported the incident.

At 6.30 a.m., a lookout woke Outerbridge again. A small submarine had been spotted just 46 metres (150 feet) from the *Ward*. The *Ward* fired its guns at the submarine and also released four depth charges (bombs inside metal drums). The submarine sank in 366 metres (1,200 feet) of water. At 6.53 a.m., Outerbridge reported

HONOR GUN

BY SINKING JAPANESE SUBMARINE ON THE MORNING OF DECEMBER 7, 1941, OFF PEARL HARBOR, THIS GUN HAS THE DISTINCTION OF BEING THE FIRST NAVAL GUN TO SPEAK AMERICA'S REPLY IN WORLD WAR II. AS SUCH, THE PEARL HARBOR ORDNANCEMEN CONSIDER IT DESERVING OF SPECIAL RESPECT AND CARE THROUGHOUT ITS LIFE.

NAME	RATE	POSITION
KNAPP, R. H.	BM2c	GUN CAPTAIN
FENTON, C. W.	Sea1c	POINTER
NOLDE, R. B.	Sea1c	TRAINER
DOMAGALL, A. A.	Sea1c	№ 1 LOADER
GRUENING, D. W.	Sea1c	№ 2 LOADER
PEICK, J. A.	Sea1c	№ 3 LOADER
FLANAGAN, H. P.	Sea1c	№ 4 LOADER
BUKREY, E. J.	GM3c	GUNNERS MATE
LASCH, K. C. J.	COX.	SIGHT SETTER

4" 50 CALIBER - GUN № 3

Japanese submarine was struck and
destroyed by crew members of the *Ward*.
A plaque was later placed on the ship's
gun, honouring the crew.

the attack to Pearl Harbor. Just seven minutes later, the *Ward* dropped four more depth charges on another submarine. "We bombed them until we ran out of depth charges and went in and got some more," he said.

Lieutenant Commander Harold Kaminsky, the radio officer on watch at Pearl Harbor, received Outerbridge's message. But Kaminsky had trouble

reaching his superior officers. When Kaminsky did reach
one of them, Captain John Earle, the officer thought the
attack was a false alarm, as several false alarms had been
reported that day. But Kaminsky believed Outerbridge's
story and kept trying to get the message to someone in
authority. He contacted the staff duty officer, who finally
reached Admiral Husband Kimmel at about 7.40 a.m.
Kimmel decided to wait to verify the accuracy of the
report. Pearl Harbor still had not been put on alert.

At 6.15 a.m., about 322 kilometres (200 miles) north
of Pearl Harbor, the 183 Japanese planes in the first
attack wave took off from their carriers. Privates Joseph
Lockard and George Elliot were operating a mobile radar
unit near the northern tip of Oahu. They were supposed
to shut it down at 7.00 a.m. The radar system was new to
the naval station, however, and Elliot wanted to practise
using it.

At 7.02 a.m., Lockard and Elliot saw a large blip on
the radar screen approaching Oahu from the north.
They believed the blip had to be a group of at least 50
planes. The men quickly called Lieutenant Kermit Tyler

at the Fort Shafter Information Centre near the harbour to report the sighting. Tyler assumed that the blip was caused by a group of 12 US B-17 bombers that was scheduled to arrive at Pearl Harbor that day. They were flying from California in the United States to help US forces in the Philippines. Tyler told Lockard and Elliot not to worry about it. Lockard and Elliot followed the blip's movement on the radar until 7.39 a.m., when it was lost in the echoes from the surrounding mountains.

Lockard and Elliot didn't realize that they, along with everyone else at Pearl Harbor, had only a few minutes left of their peaceful Sunday morning. Life at the naval base – and for the whole United States – was about to change forever.

THE B-17S

At first, the approaching Japanese warplanes were believed to be 12 US B-17 bombers that had been expected to arrive at Pearl Harbor on 7 December. The planes made it to Pearl Harbor that morning as scheduled, then flew into the Hickam Field air base in the middle of the Japanese attack!

To minimize flying weight, the B-17s were unarmed, so their pilots couldn't join in the defence of the base. It was all they could do to try to land while taking fire from Japanese planes and from confused US troops on the ground. Luckily, the pilots managed to land their planes, many covered with bullet holes, at locations across Oahu, including a golf course. One plane split into two as it landed, but all of the pilots survived.

US B-17 bomber used during World War II

PRESIDENT ROOSEVELT AND PEARL HARBOR

Some people think top US government leaders knew that the Japanese were going to attack Pearl Harbor. Most historians believe President Franklin D. Roosevelt was eager for the United States to enter the war. But they don't believe he purposely refused to take action to avoid the attack. The signs warning of an attack on Pearl Harbor were either misunderstood or came too late to help.

The president knew the huge threat that Axis powers posed to the United States and the rest of the world. And in 1941 the US economy and the people were still recovering from the devastating effects of the Great Depression (1929-1939). During the 1930s Roosevelt had established government programmes designed to help the unemployed, but many people were still living in poverty. If the United States entered the war, the huge need for weapons and other war materials would put many people to work and boost the economy.

Conspiracy theorists who believe Roosevelt wanted Japan to attack the United States – thus forcing the United States to declare war – point to the fact that the entire Pacific Fleet was headquartered at

President Roosevelt addressed the public on 8 December 1941, regarding the attack on Pearl Harbor.

Pearl Harbor: a location that was open to attack from all sides. But according to historian Craig Shirley, the author of a book about the Pearl Harbor attack, "neither Roosevelt nor anybody in his government, the Navy or the War Department knew that the Japanese were going to attack Pearl Harbor. There was no conspiracy."

Six large aircraft carriers were used to transport the more than 350 planes the Japanese used in their attack on Pearl Harbor.

CHAPTER FIVE

TORA, TORA, TORA

The Japanese strike force stopped to regroup about 1,046 kilometres (650 miles) north of Pearl Harbor on 6 December. The carriers then sailed rapidly towards the launch point that had been chosen for the attack, about 322 kilometres (200 miles) north of Oahu. They reached the launch point at about 3.00 a.m. on 7 December.

All members of the Japanese strike force were prepared to die during the attack on Pearl Harbor. They were proud to give their lives for their country. As they waited for the attack to begin, many of the men prayed, while others wrote letters to their families in case they didn't survive. Some enclosed locks of hair and even fingernail clippings with their letters. The men knew that if they died in the attack, their bodies would probably be lost at sea. They wanted to leave their families something by which to remember them.

In the hours before dawn, the Japanese pilots got ready for their mission. They ate a ceremonial breakfast of *sekhan*, a dish made of rice and beans served at special occasions, and Japanese wine called sake. Some crew members wore a belt called a *senninbari*, which means "thousand stitch". The cloth belts were covered with 1,000 thread knots embroidered by 1,000 people who wished the crew members good luck. The pilots tied bandannas called *hachimakis* around their heads. Written on each hachimaki was the word *hissho*, which means "certain victory".

a senninbari

Japanese pilots were given instructions before taking off for Pearl Harbor.

As the air attack commander, Captain Mitsuo
Fuchida wore a special *hachimaki* given to him by the
crew of the *Akagi*. He also wore red underwear and a red
shirt. Fuchida thought that if he were wounded, the red
clothing would hide the blood from his men. Then they
could concentrate on their mission rather than worrying
about him.

Two seaplanes flew off to scout the planned route to
Oahu at 5.30 a.m. The weather wasn't good for flying.
The wind speed was high and the sea was rough,
sending waves crashing over the aircraft carrier decks.

Crewmen held the aeroplanes to keep them from going overboard. The carriers turned into the wind, and at 6.10 a.m., the *Akagi* raised its battle flag. A lamp on the ship's flight deck shone green, giving the signal for the planes to take off.

Mitsuo Fuchida's Nakajima B5N2 horizontal bomber took off first to lead the attack. A group of 183 planes

The crew of a Japanese aircraft carrier cheered as the pilots in the first attack wave took off.

formed the first wave. They included torpedo bombers, dive bombers, horizontal bombers and fighter planes. The fighter planes would protect the torpedo planes and bombers.

The entire first wave was in the air by 6.15 a.m. As soon as the first group of planes left each carrier deck, a second wave was brought up. The entire attack force included about 350 planes.

Fuchida used a Honolulu radio station to check his course. As he zeroed in on the signal, he noticed that the station was playing music. That told him that the Americans had no idea an attack was coming. "One hour and forty minutes after leaving the carriers I knew that we should be nearing our goal. Small openings in the thick cloud cover afforded occasional glimpses of the ocean, as I strained my eyes for the first sight of land. Suddenly a long white line of breaking surf appeared directly beneath my plane. It was the northern shore of Oahu," Fuchida wrote later.

As the US fleet came into Fuchida's view, he was disappointed to see no aircraft carriers anchored with the other ships. All of the US carriers were elsewhere that day. The *Enterprise* had been sent to carry fighter planes to Wake Island. The *Lexington* was transporting bombers to Midway Island. The *Saratoga* had just been repaired on the west coast of the United States, and the *Yorktown* wasn't yet ready for combat. The absence of

Photos taken from a Japanese bomber show the destruction of Pearl Harbor as the attack unfolded.

the aircraft carriers was a stroke of luck for the United States. During the war, the US carriers would play a huge role in combat, especially in the Pacific.

Fuchida ordered a radio operator to send the signal "To, to, to!" to his pilots at 7.49 a.m. *To* is the first syllable of *totsugeki* – the Japanese word for "charge" or "attack". Minutes later the operator completed the message: "To ra, to ra, to ra!" The full message meant "Attack, surprise achieved."

About six minutes later, lead dive-bomber pilot Kukuichi Takahashi dropped the first bomb on a seaplane ramp at the Naval Air Station on Ford Island. The attack had begun.

TOO LATE

Admiral Yamamoto wanted to give the United States a warning, but Japan's Prime Minister Hideki Tojo, who wanted a surprise attack, overruled him. Tojo did agree to a slight compromise, though. US Secretary of State Cordell Hull would be notified at 1.00 p.m. Washington, DC, time on 7 December that Japan was breaking off peace talks. That time was 7.30 a.m. in Hawaii – just 30 minutes before the attack on Pearl Harbor and too late for the US military to prevent the attack.

Pearl Harbor filled with smoke from the burning US battleships bombed during the attack.

CHAPTER SIX

NOT A DRILL

Rear Admiral William Furlong was standing on the deck of the minelayer USS *Oglala* at 7.55 a.m. when he saw the seaplane ramp explode into splinters. As he got a closer look at the low-flying bomber, he saw the emblem of the Japanese flag – a rising red sun – on its wings.

At the same time, Lieutenant Commander Logan Ramsey saw the low-flying bomber through the window of the Ford Island Command Centre. His first thought was that it was a reckless US pilot. Then he saw "something black fall out of that plane". Realizing it was a bomb, he ran to the radio room and ordered the operators to immediately send out an uncoded message on all frequencies: "AIR RAID ON PEARL

HARBOR. THIS IS NOT DRILL." The message went out at 7.58 a.m. to Pearl Harbor's commander, Admiral Husband Kimmel, as well as to government officials in Washington, DC, and to the headquarters of the US Asiatic Fleet in the Philippines.

More than 90 ships were anchored in Pearl Harbor at the time of the attack. Because the aircraft carriers weren't there, the nine battleships were the Japanese pilots' primary targets. During the first few minutes of the attack, bombs or torpedoes struck all the battleships next to Ford Island.

Hangars at the Ford Island Naval Air Station seaplane base were also targeted. The attack left many of the planes in ruins.

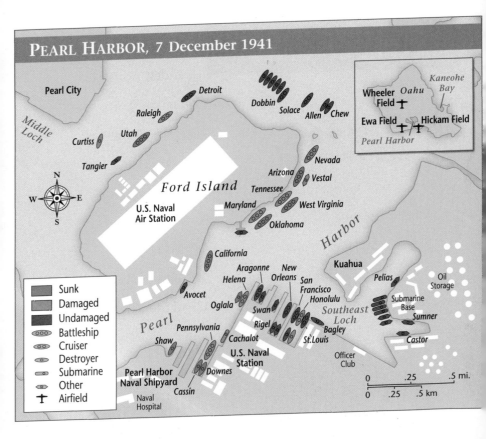

PEARL HARBOR, 7 December 1941

Some Japanese planes attacked from just 15 metres (50 feet) in the air. They dropped torpedoes that travelled through the water and exploded when they hit a ship. Horizontal bombers dropped bombs from high in the air, out of reach of anti-aircraft guns. Dive-bombers flew high and then dived to drop their bombs.

A LONE DEFENDER

The naval station at Kaneohe Bay, about 20 kilometres (12 miles) north-east of Honolulu, was the first US military base to come under attack on 7 December. Chief Petty Officer John Finn, who was in charge of munitions at Kaneohe Bay, was still in bed when he heard the sounds of aeroplanes and machine guns.

Finn dressed, jumped into his car, and raced to the hangar. Japanese planes flew above him. When he reached the airstrip, Finn found there were no anti-aircraft guns or mounts for the machine guns.

Finn had to think quickly. He picked up a machine gun, a tripod and ammunition and dragged it all about 20 metres (60 feet) out onto the runway. From there he spent the next two hours shooting at Japanese planes. Even though shrapnel hit him more than 20 times, he kept shooting.

"I got shot in the left arm and shot in the left foot, broke the bone," he said later. "I had shrapnel blows in my chest and belly and right elbow and right thumb. Some were just scratches. My scalp got cut, and everybody thought I was dying. I had 28, 29 holes in me that were bleeding."

The Japanese pilots destroyed all but 6 of the 33 seaplane patrol boats at Kaneohe Bay, and they killed 18 men. Finn was credited with

A burial ceremony of 15 officers and men killed at Kaneohe Bay took place on 8 December 1941.

shooting down at least one Japanese plane. He was one of 15 servicemen awarded the US Medal of Honor for his actions that day. Only five of the recipients survived the attack. Finn remained in the navy and rose to the rank of lieutenant in 1944. He died in 2010 at the age of 100.

That morning 1,512 men were aboard the *Arizona*. Many were sleeping or eating breakfast when the explosions began. The general quarters alarm sounded. That meant that all crew members had to immediately report to their battle stations. But there was a problem. Because it was Sunday, none of the ship's anti-aircraft guns were loaded, and the ammunition was locked up. One sailor used a metal tool to break open the padlock of an ammunition compartment. He handed ammunition to the other crew members as they raced to their battle stations.

Before the *Arizona*'s crew could fire the anti-aircraft guns, 10 Japanese Nakajima B5N bomber planes attacked. The planes dropped five bombs on the ship's deck and an armour-piercing bomb on the forward ammunition magazine. All the ammunition stored there exploded, along with the front part of the ship. The explosion blew some men off the decks of the *Arizona* and nearby ships. Being thrown free of a burning ship saved some sailors from death. After the explosion, what was left of the *Arizona* quickly sank in the harbour.